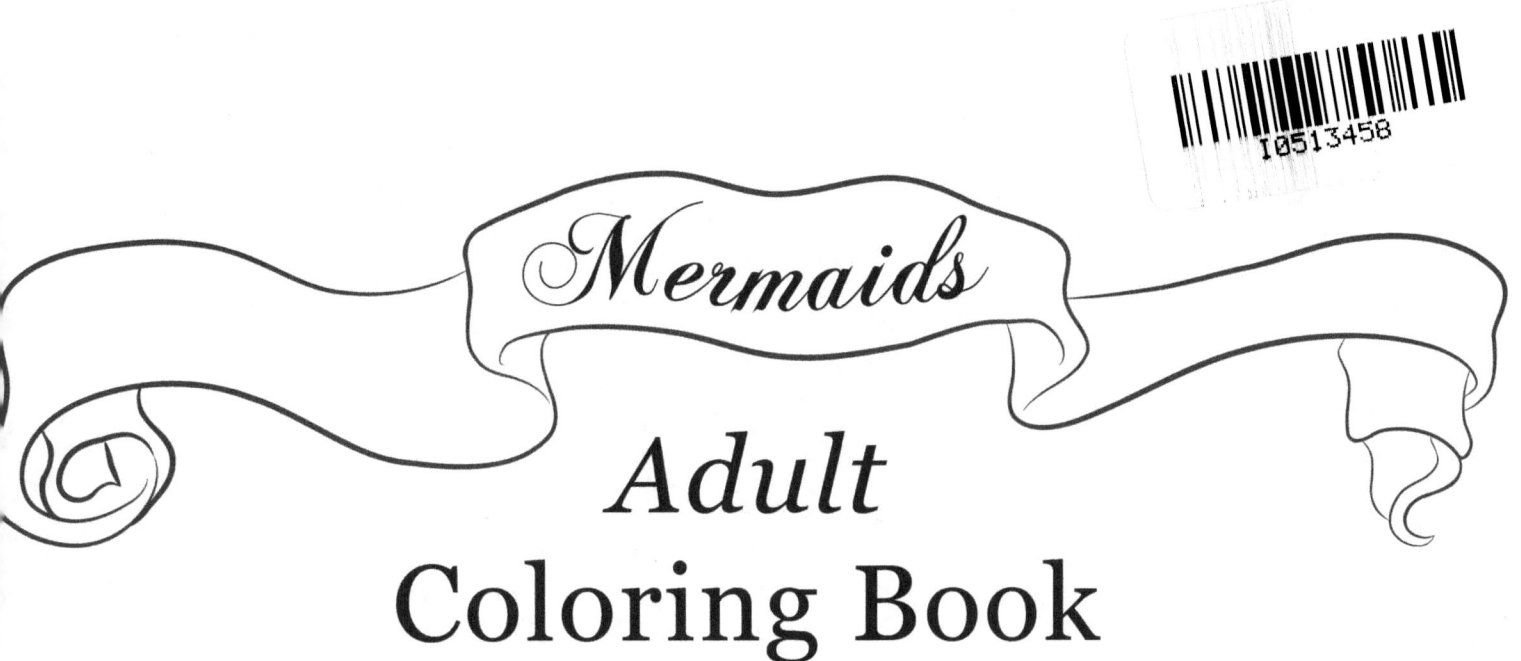

Mermaids
Adult Coloring Book

Swim and be free, the singing muses of the sea.

Jake Anthony

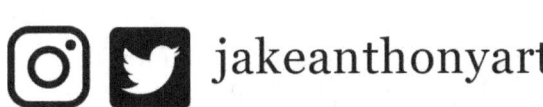 jakeanthonyart

Copyright © 2018
by Jake Anthony.

All rights reserved under
International and Pan American
Copyright Conventions.

Color Test

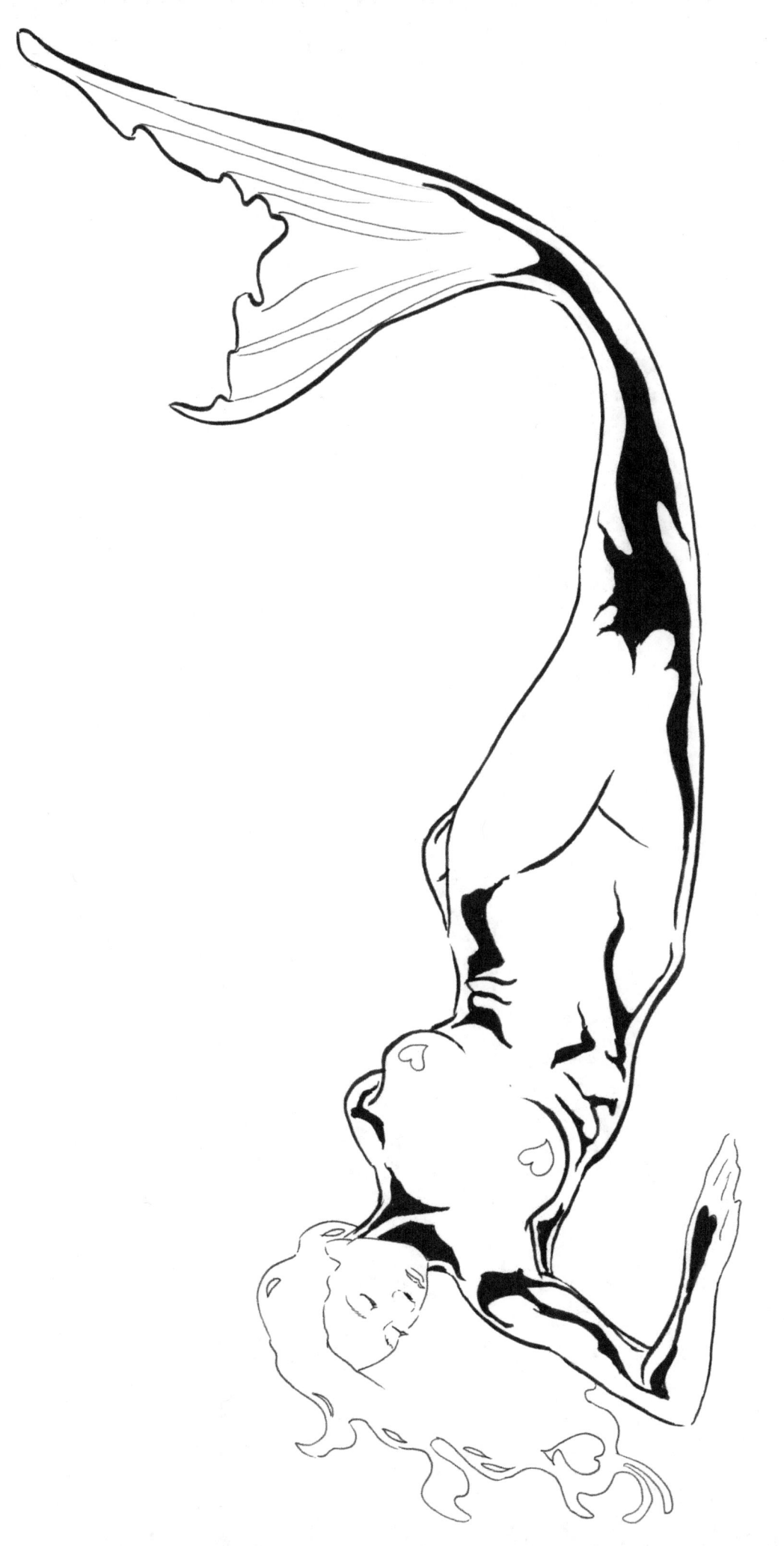

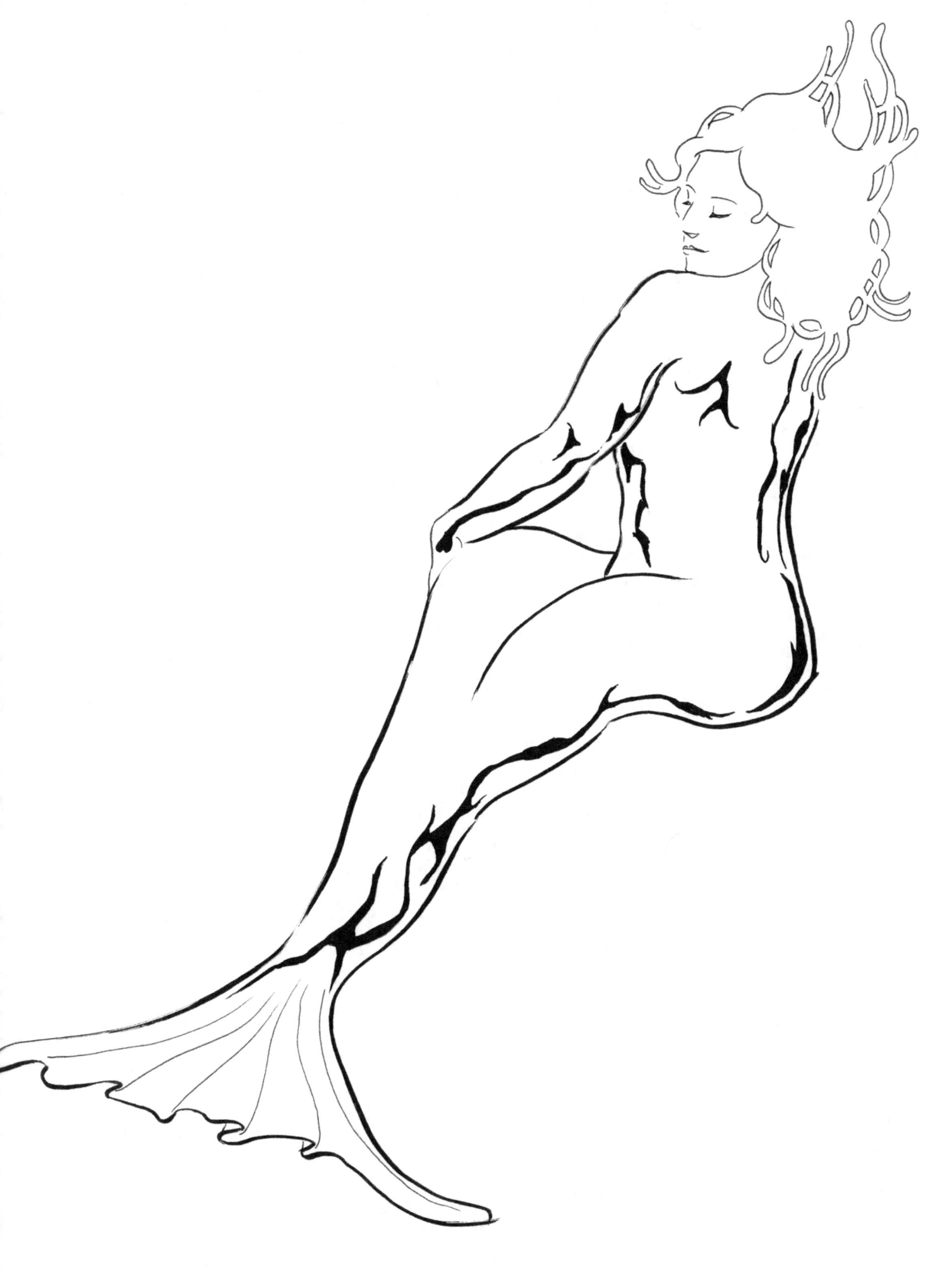

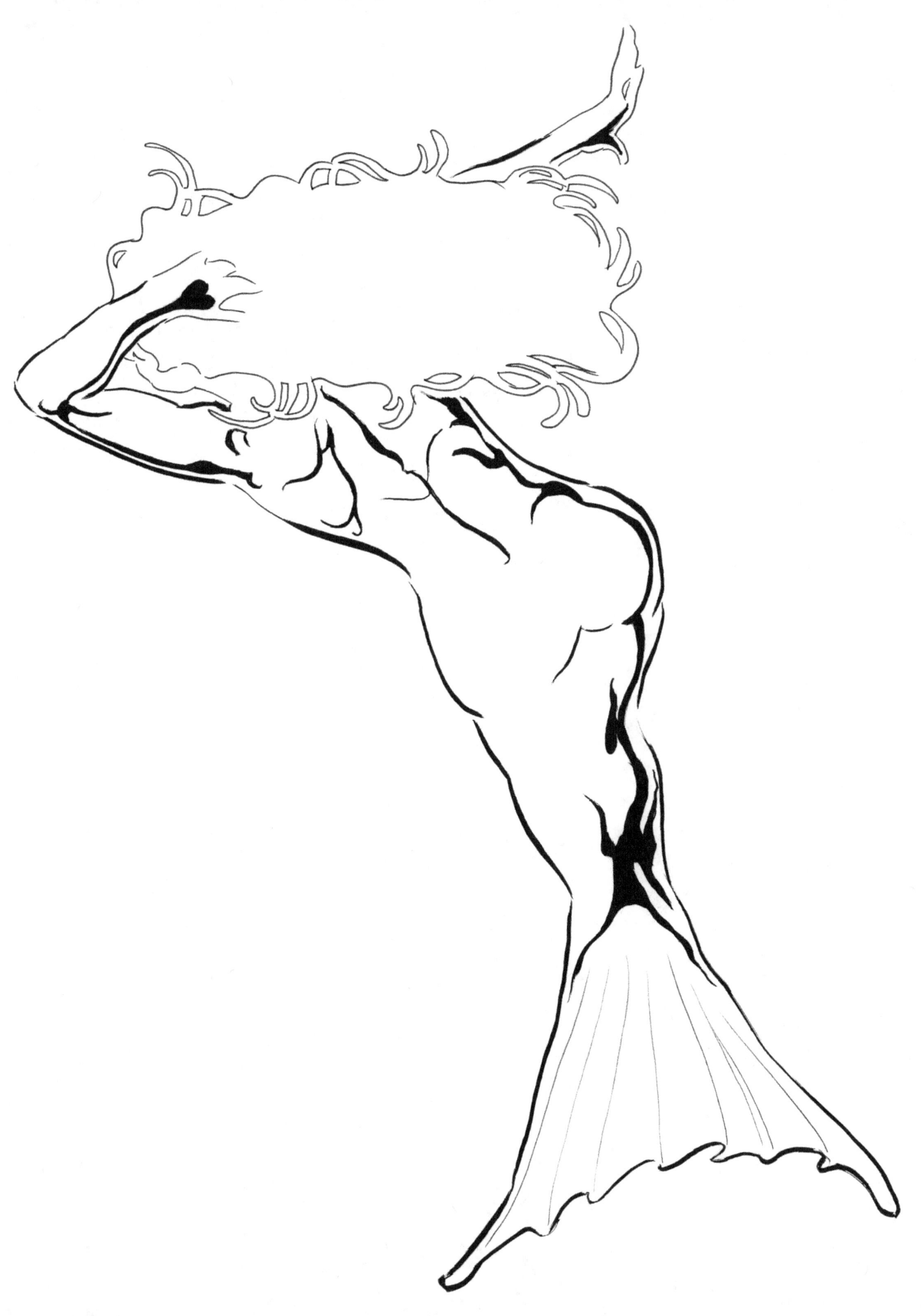

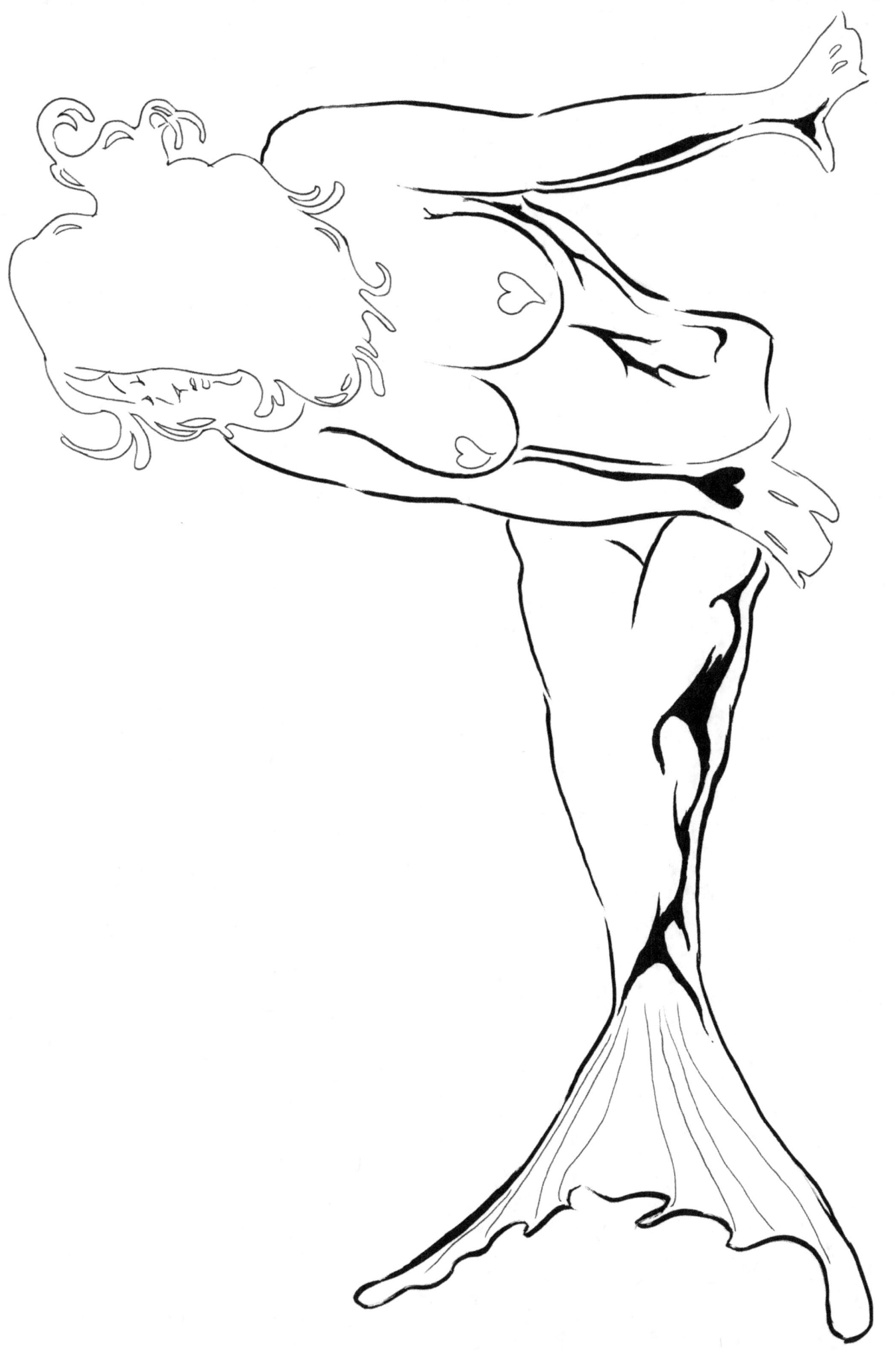

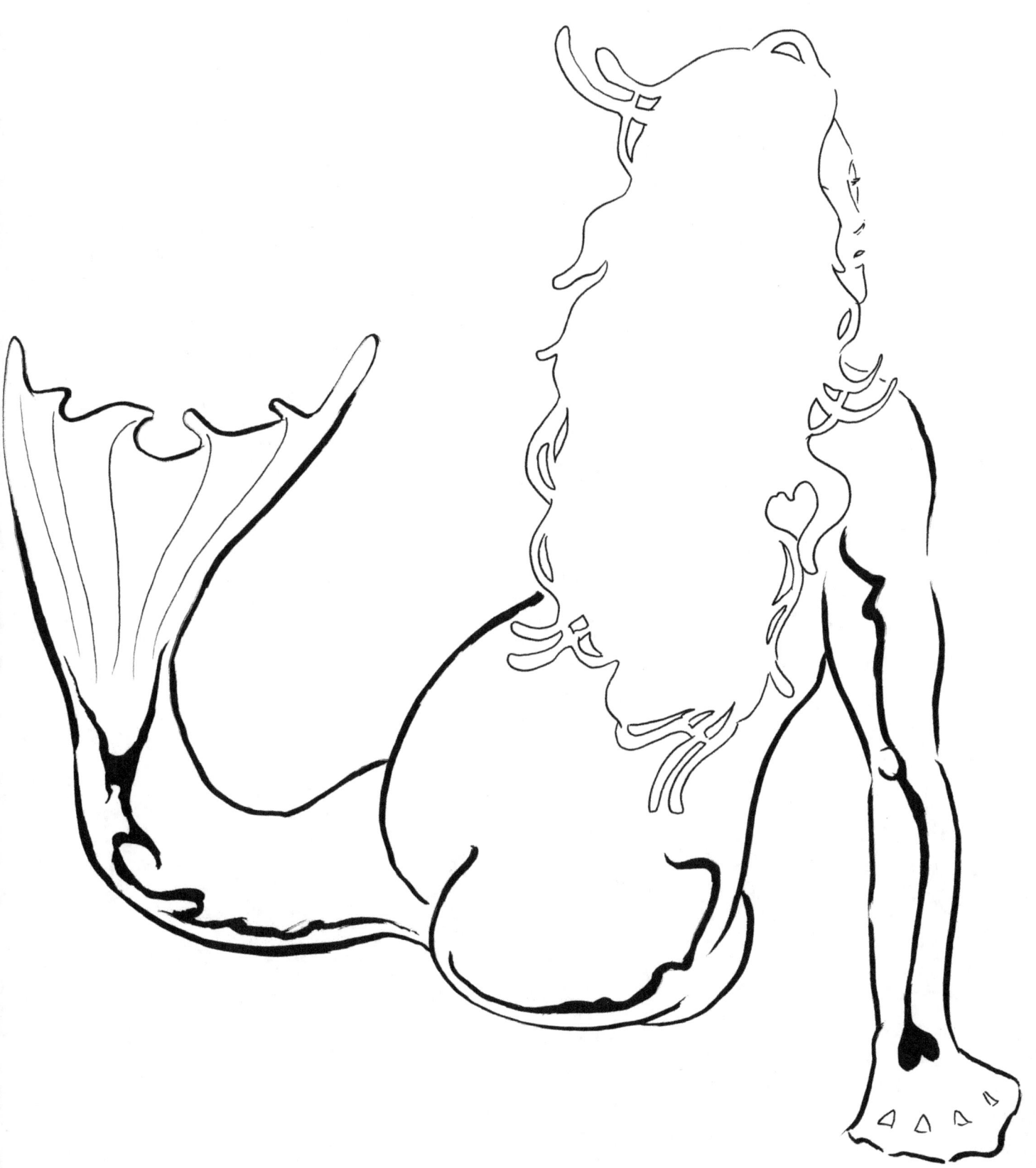

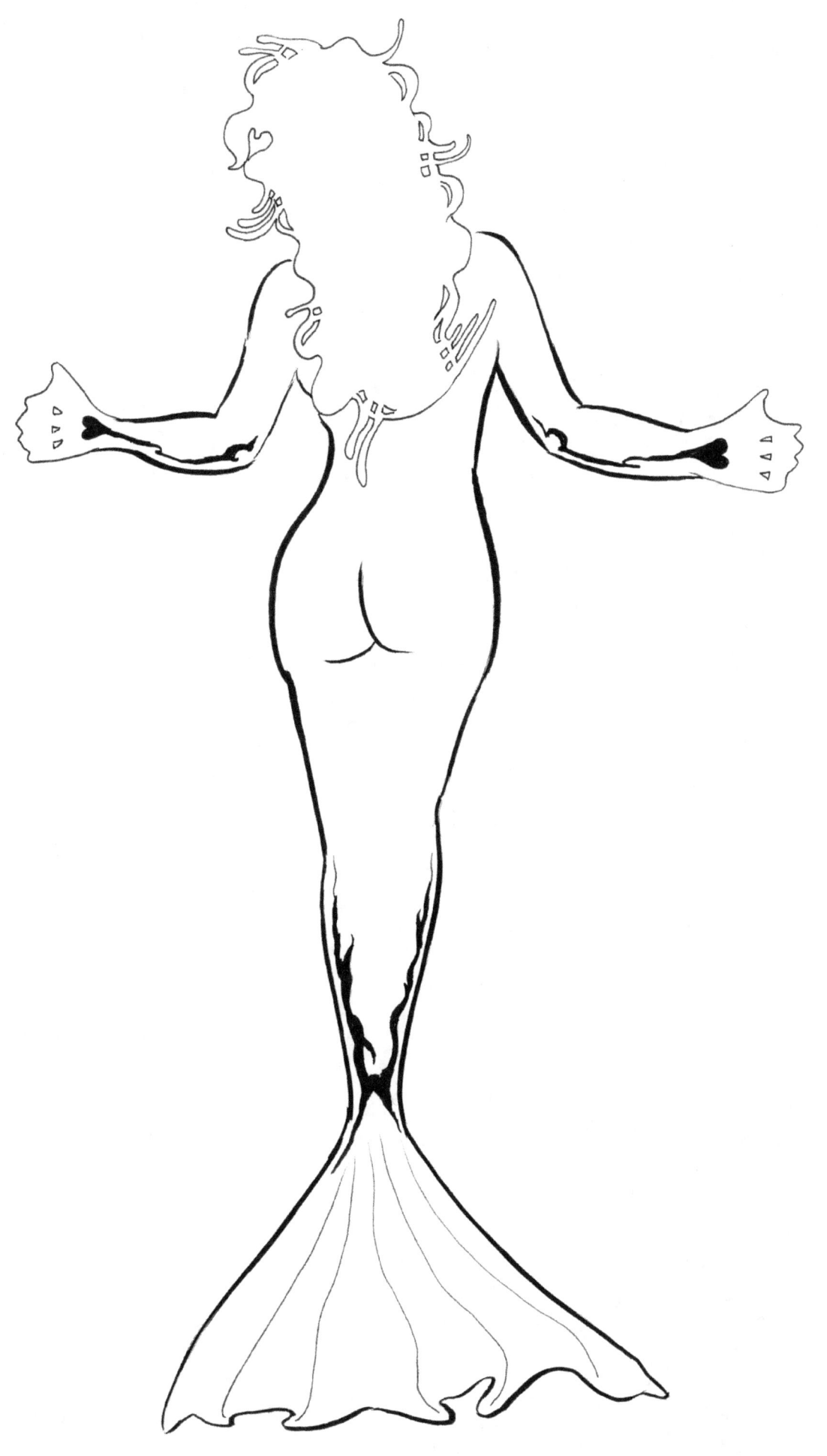

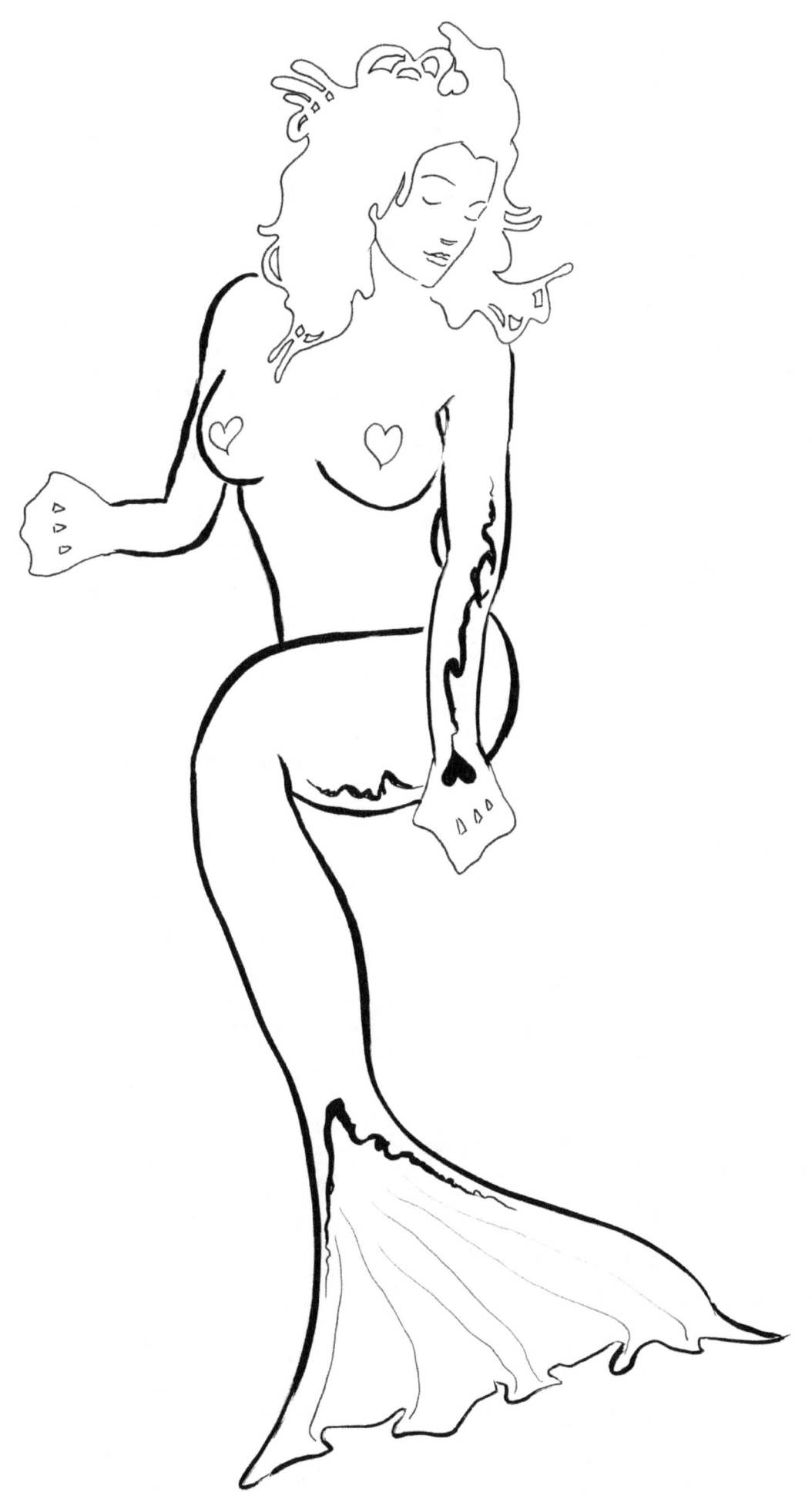

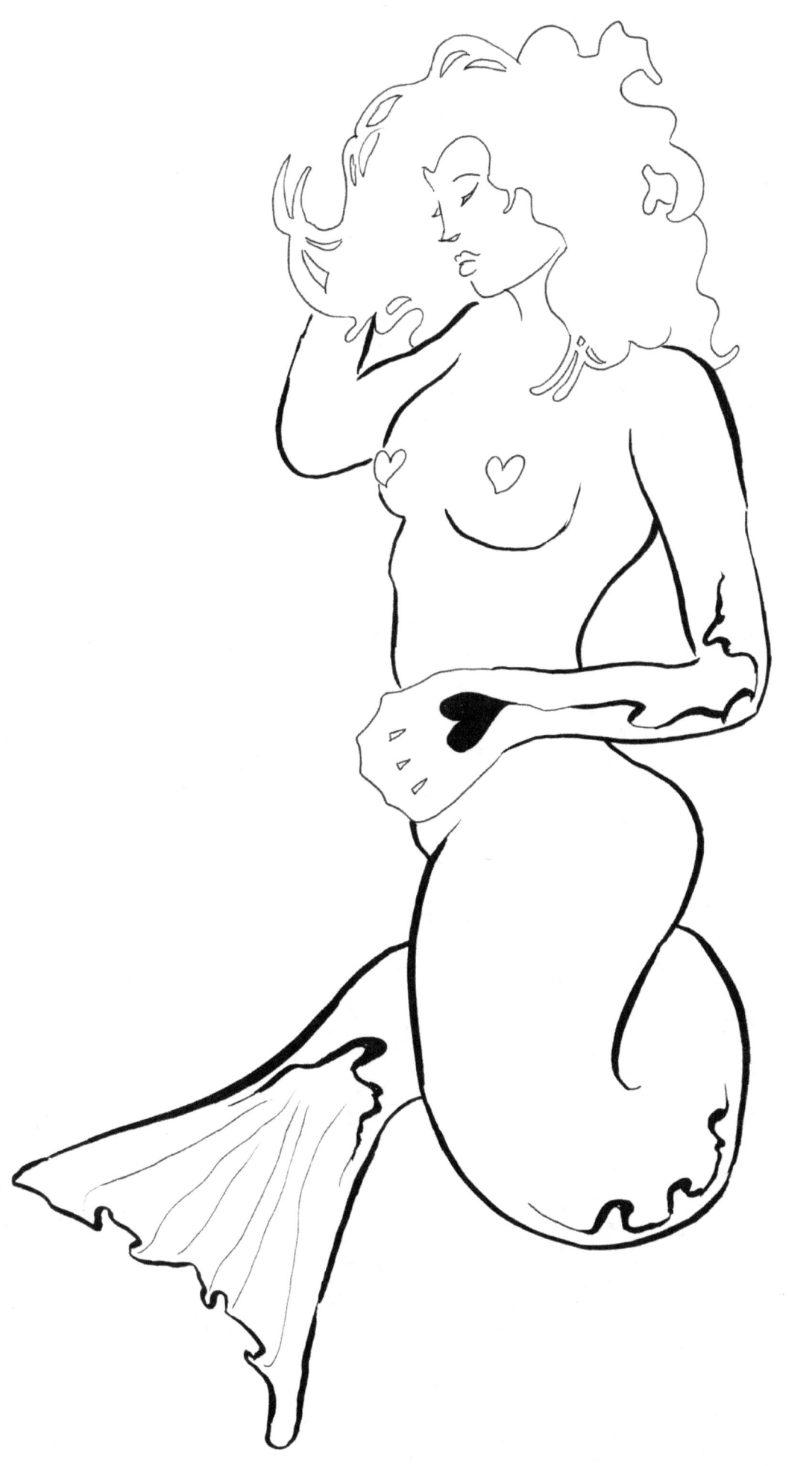

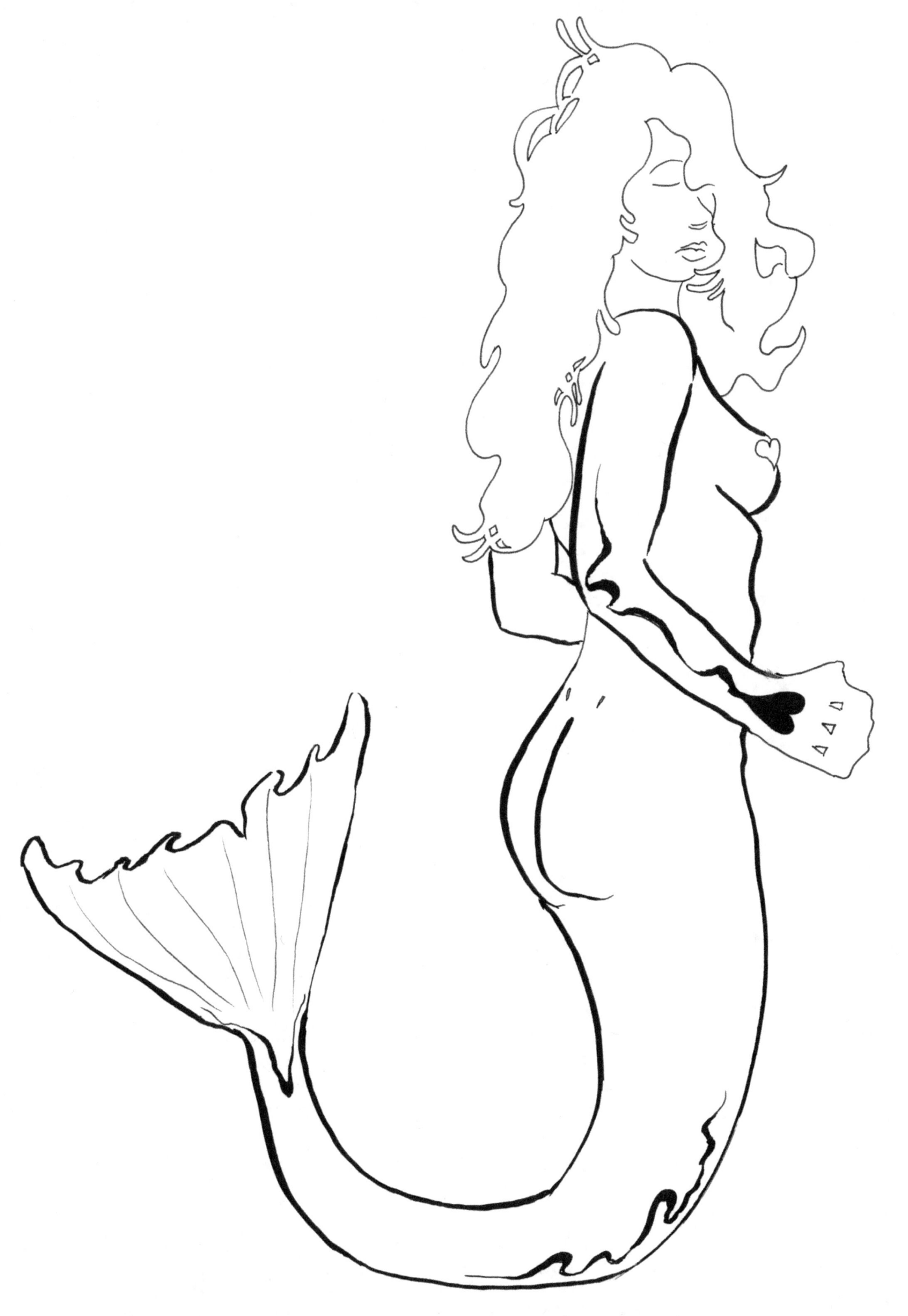

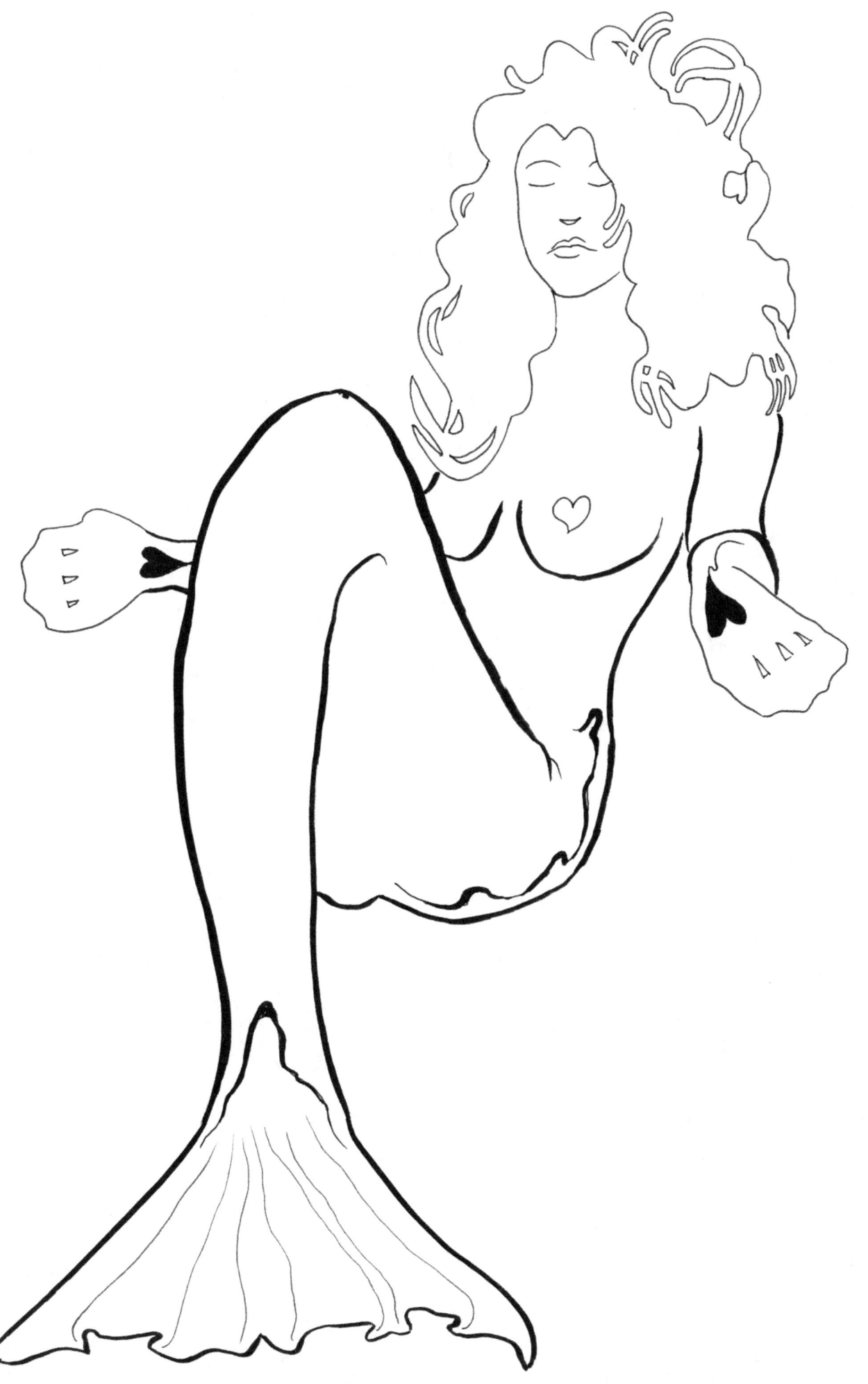

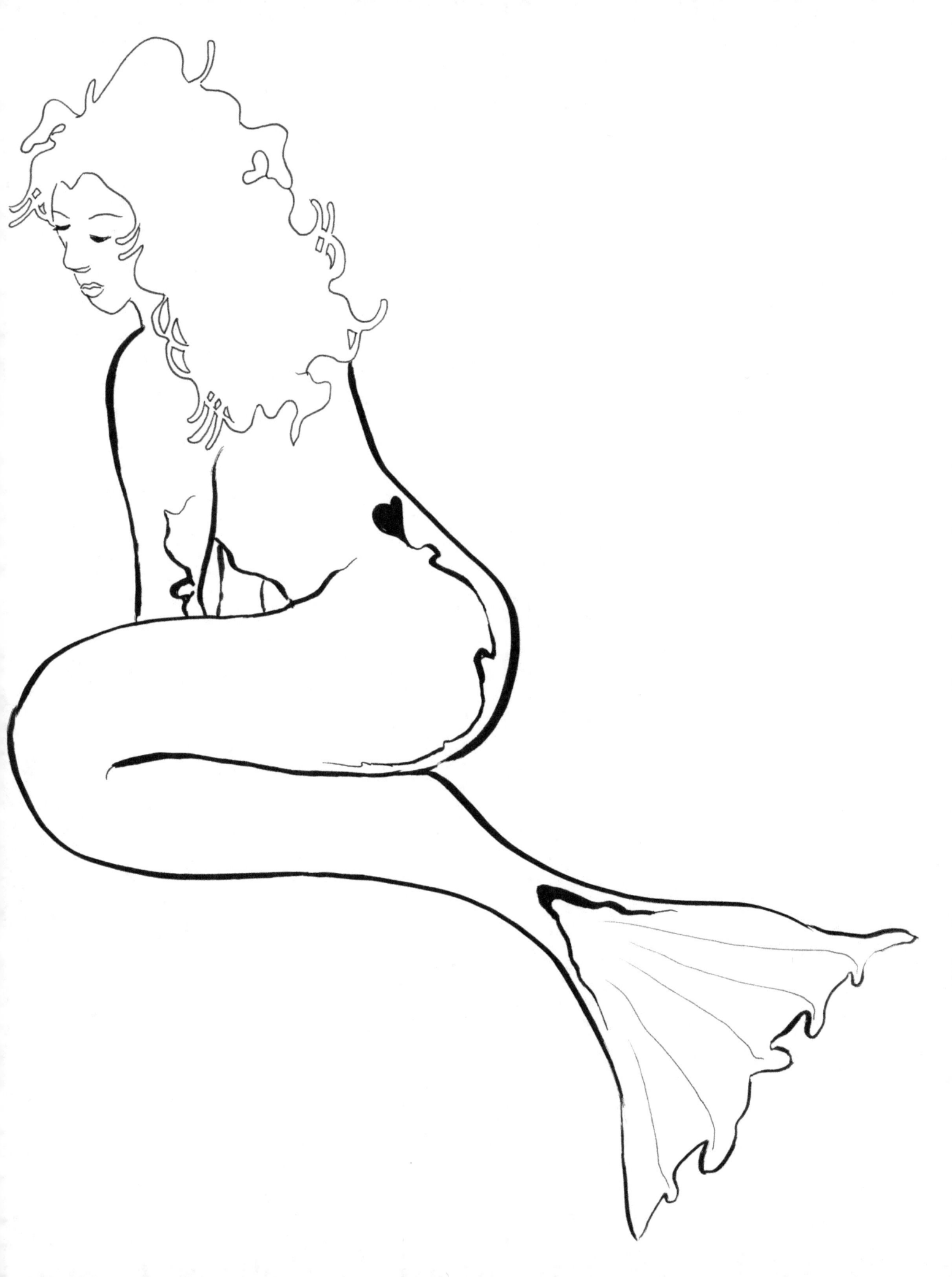

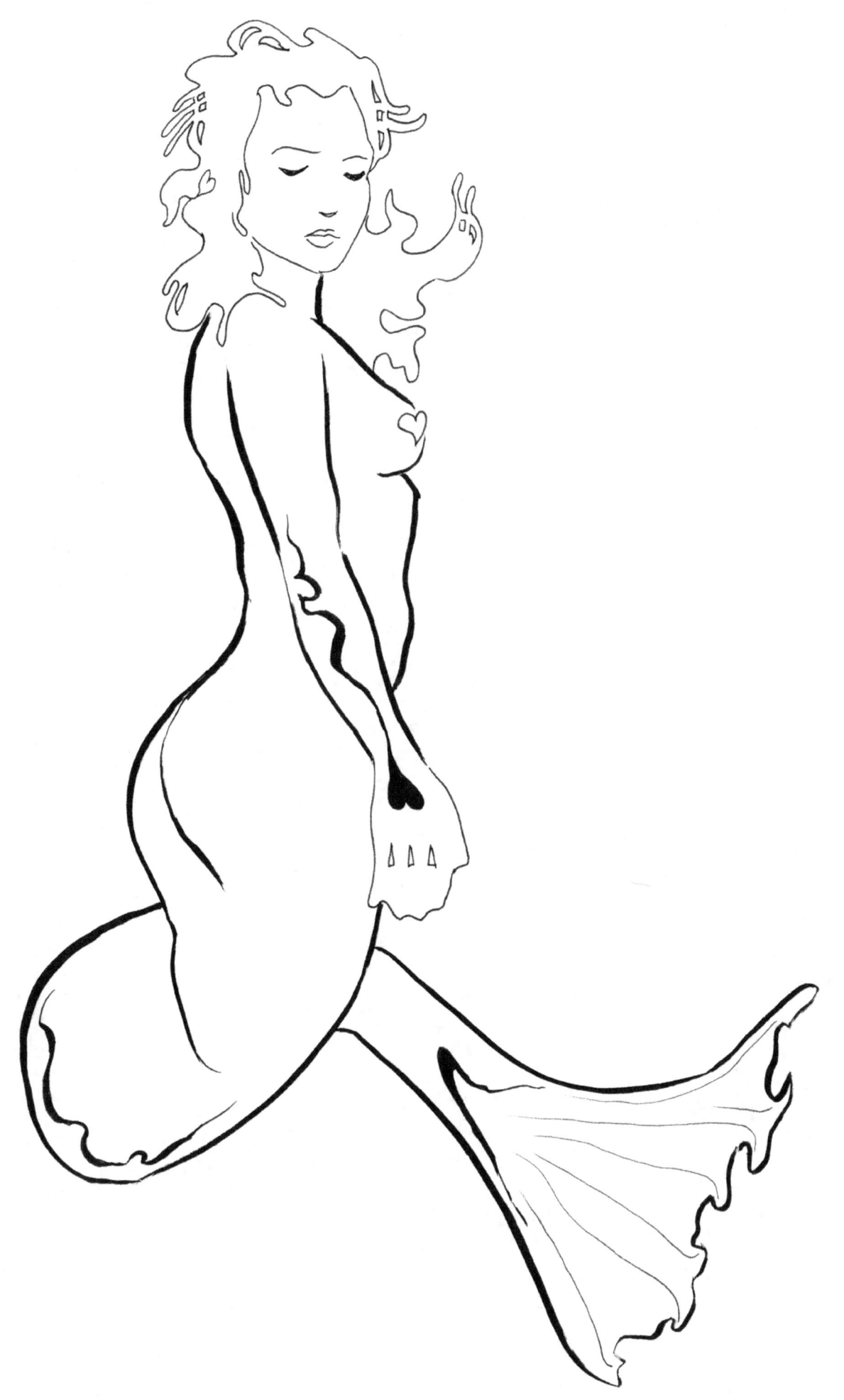

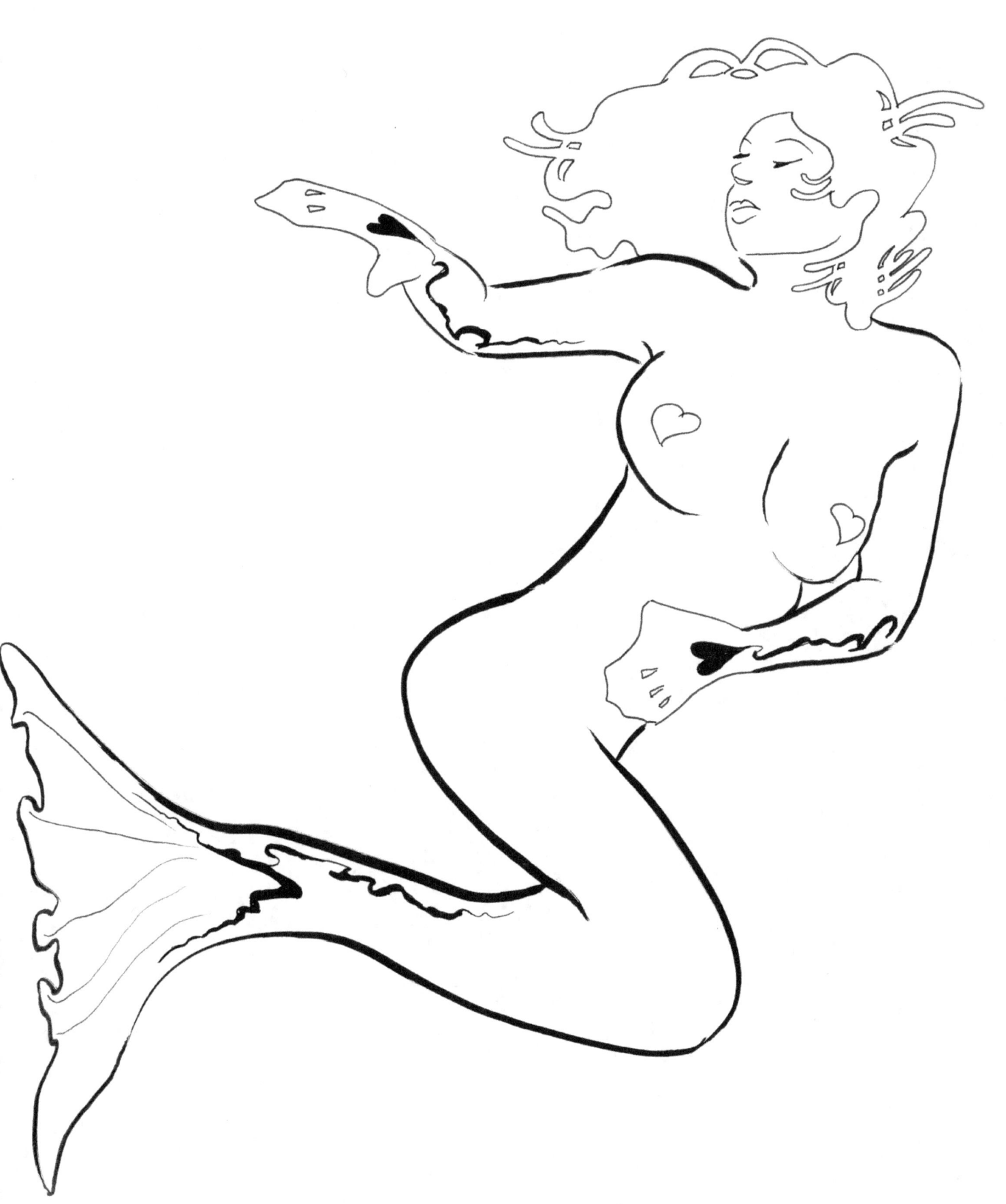

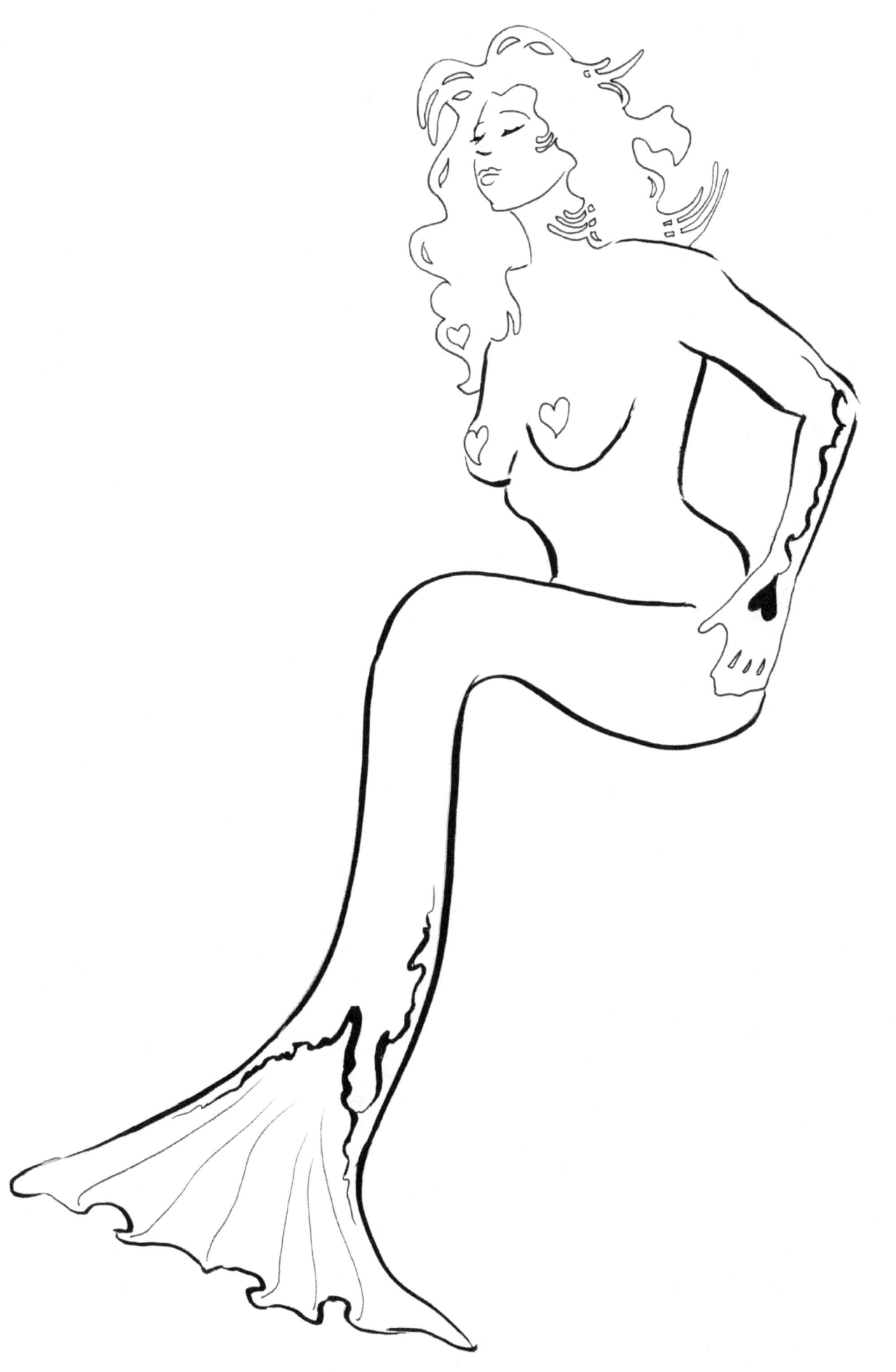

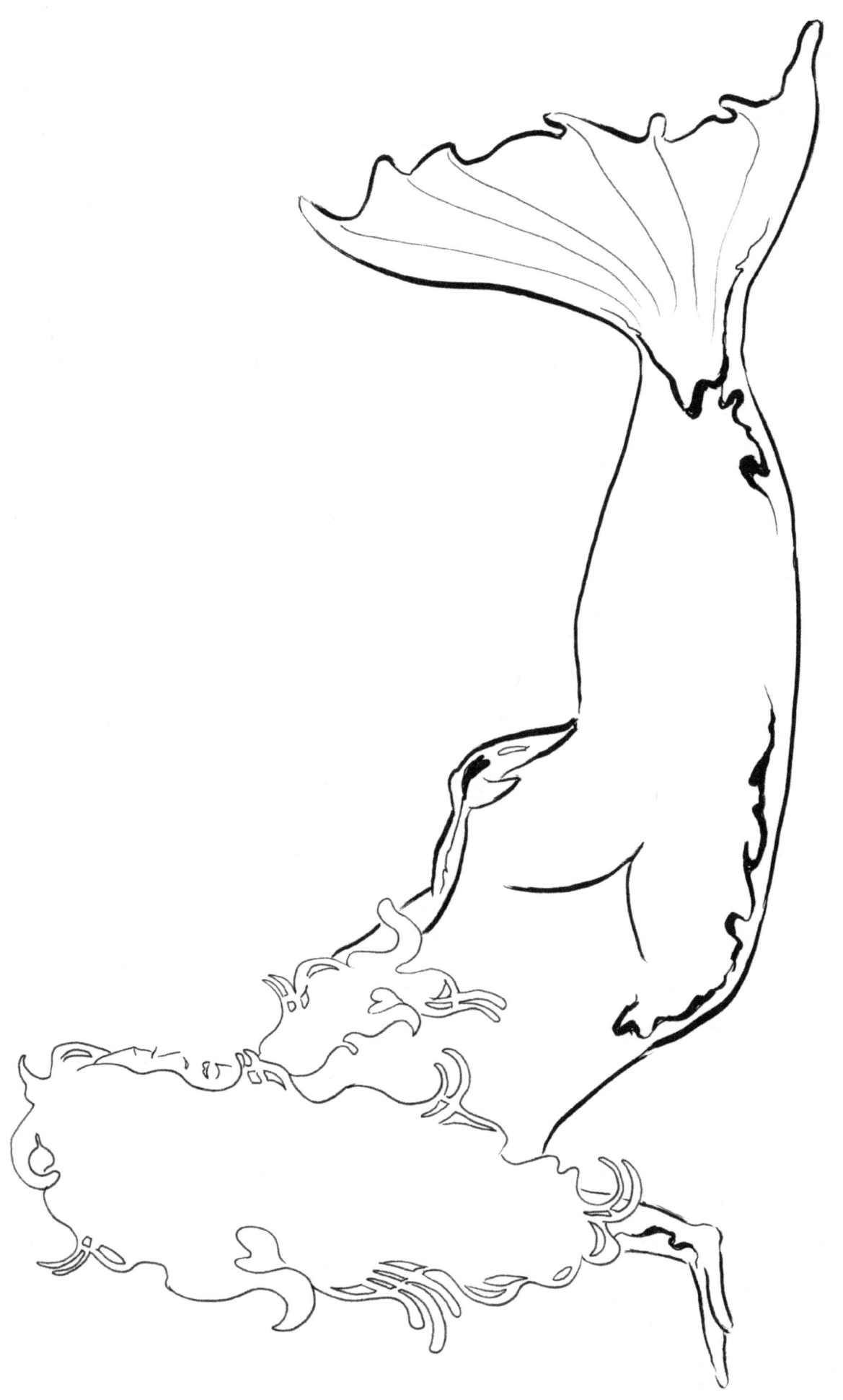

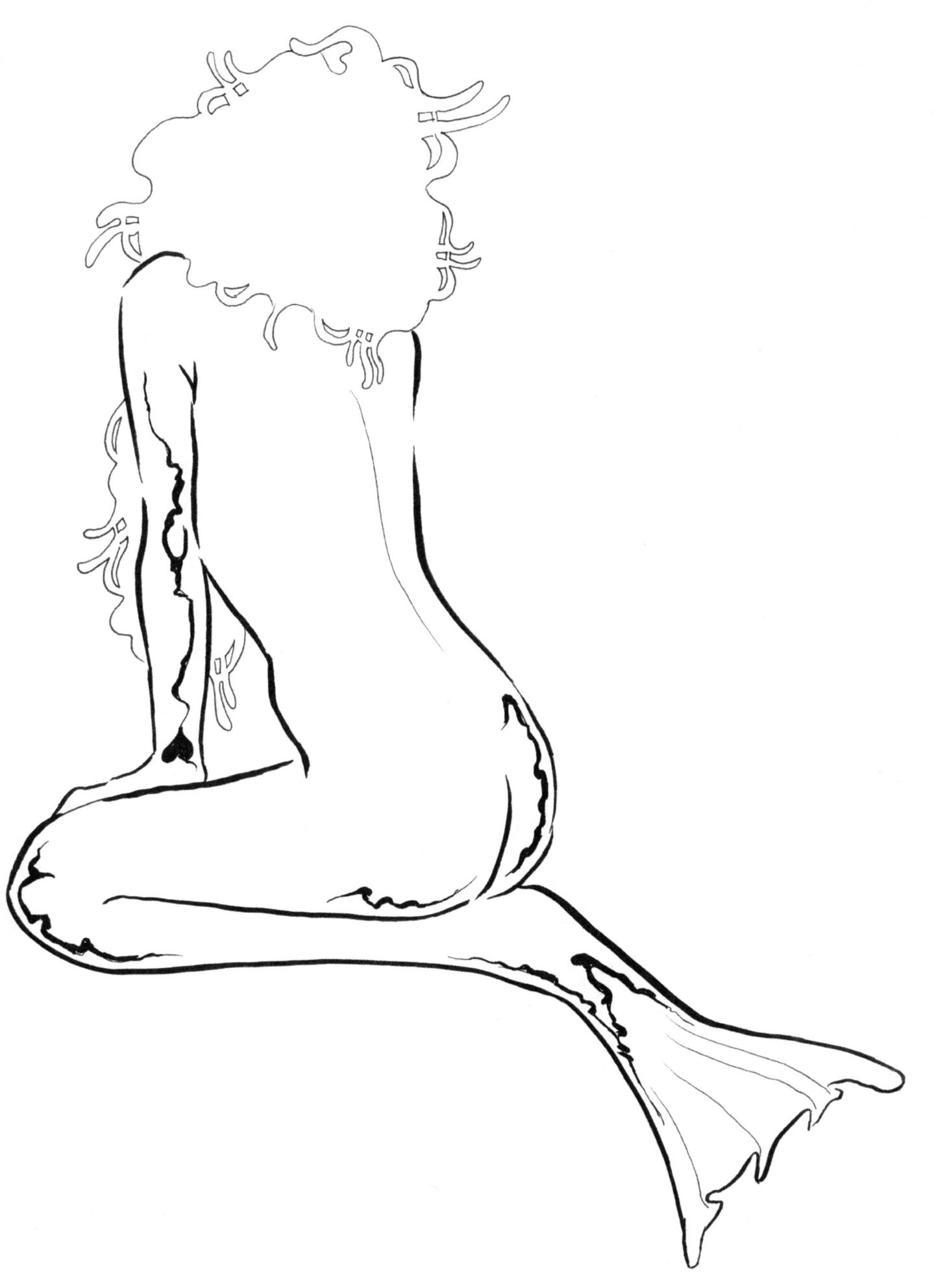

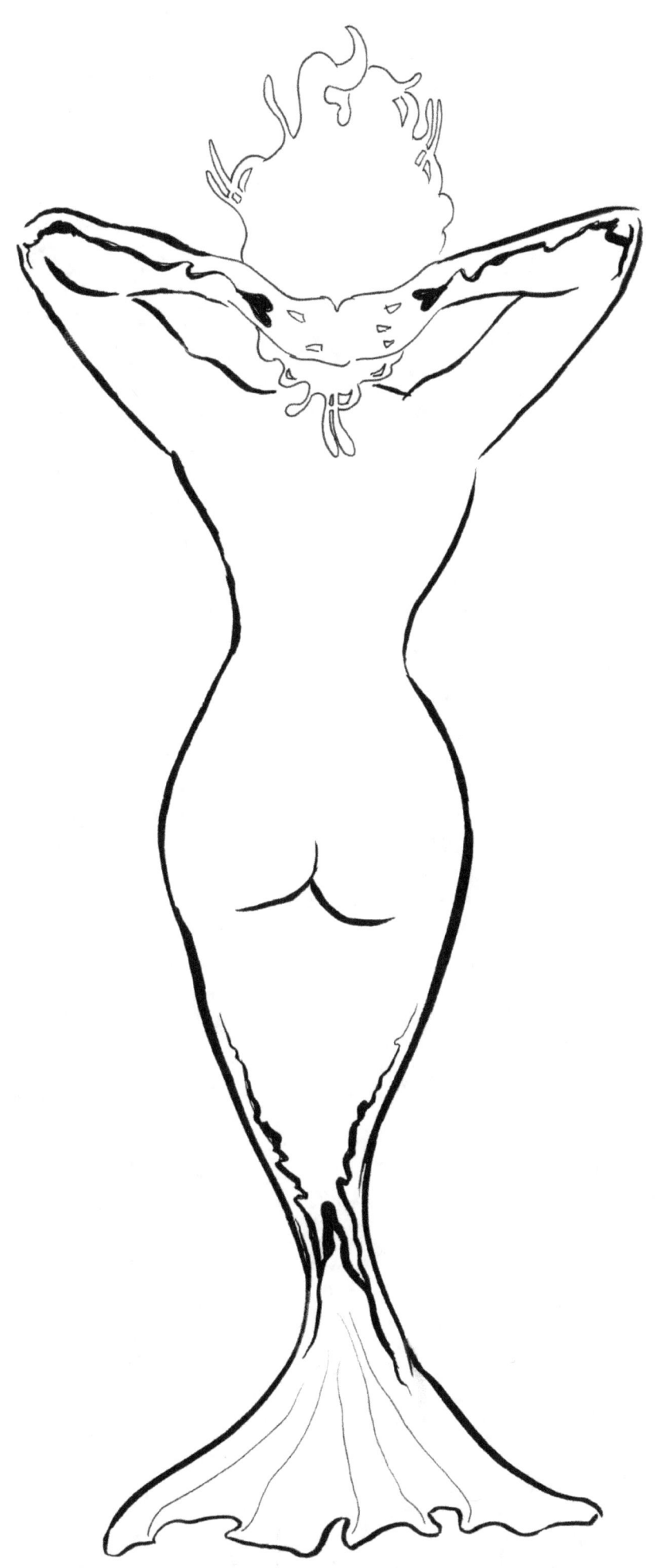

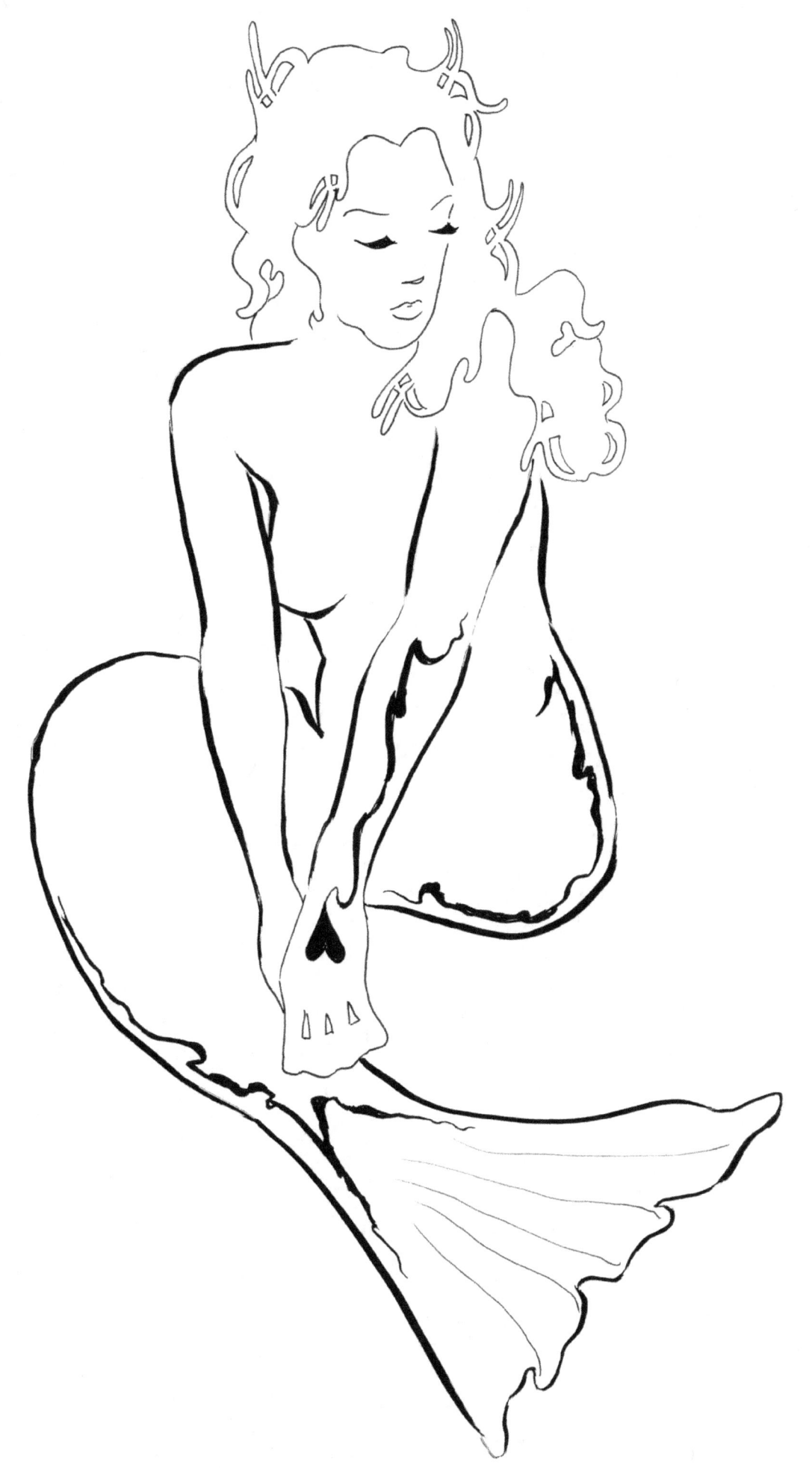

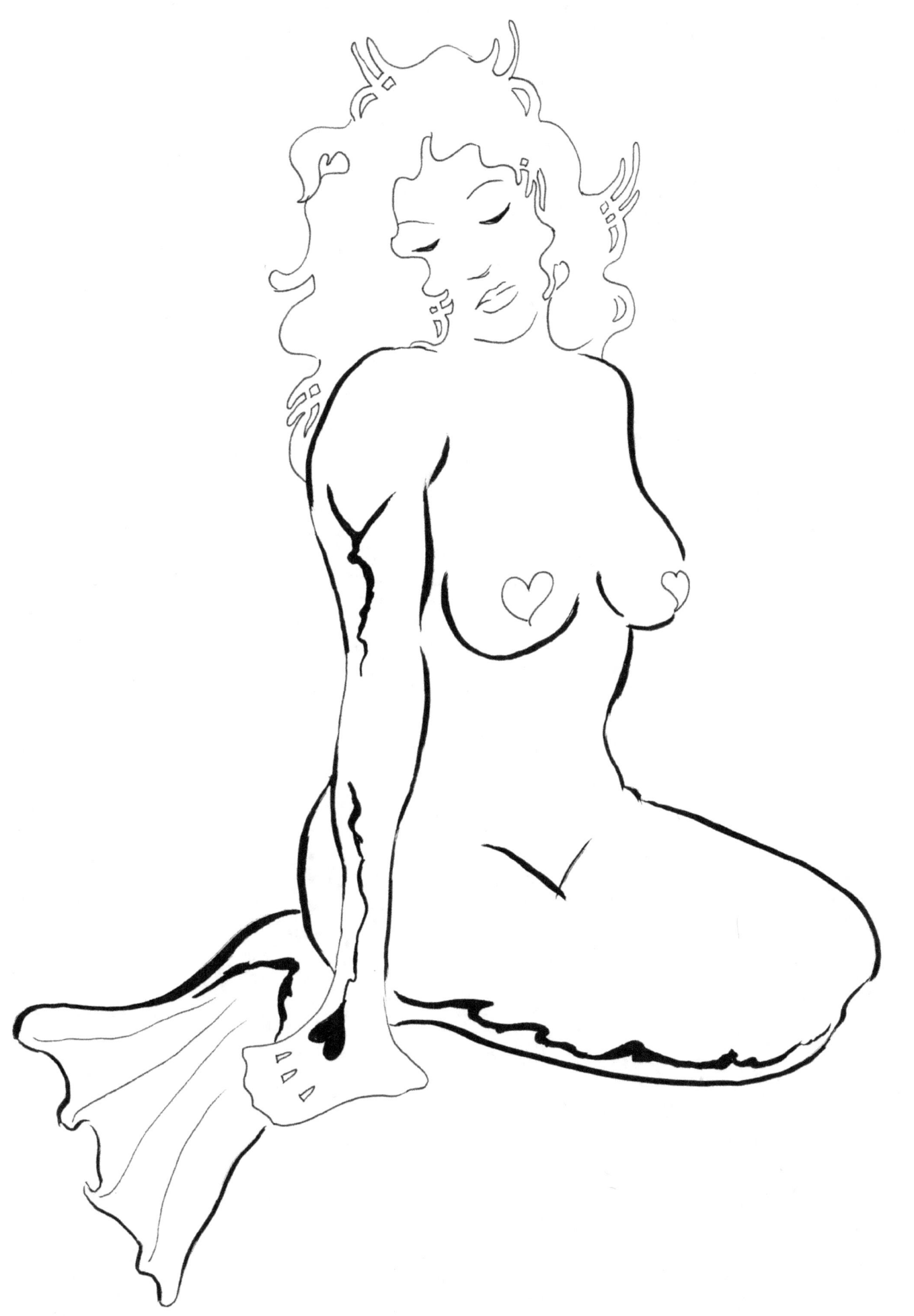

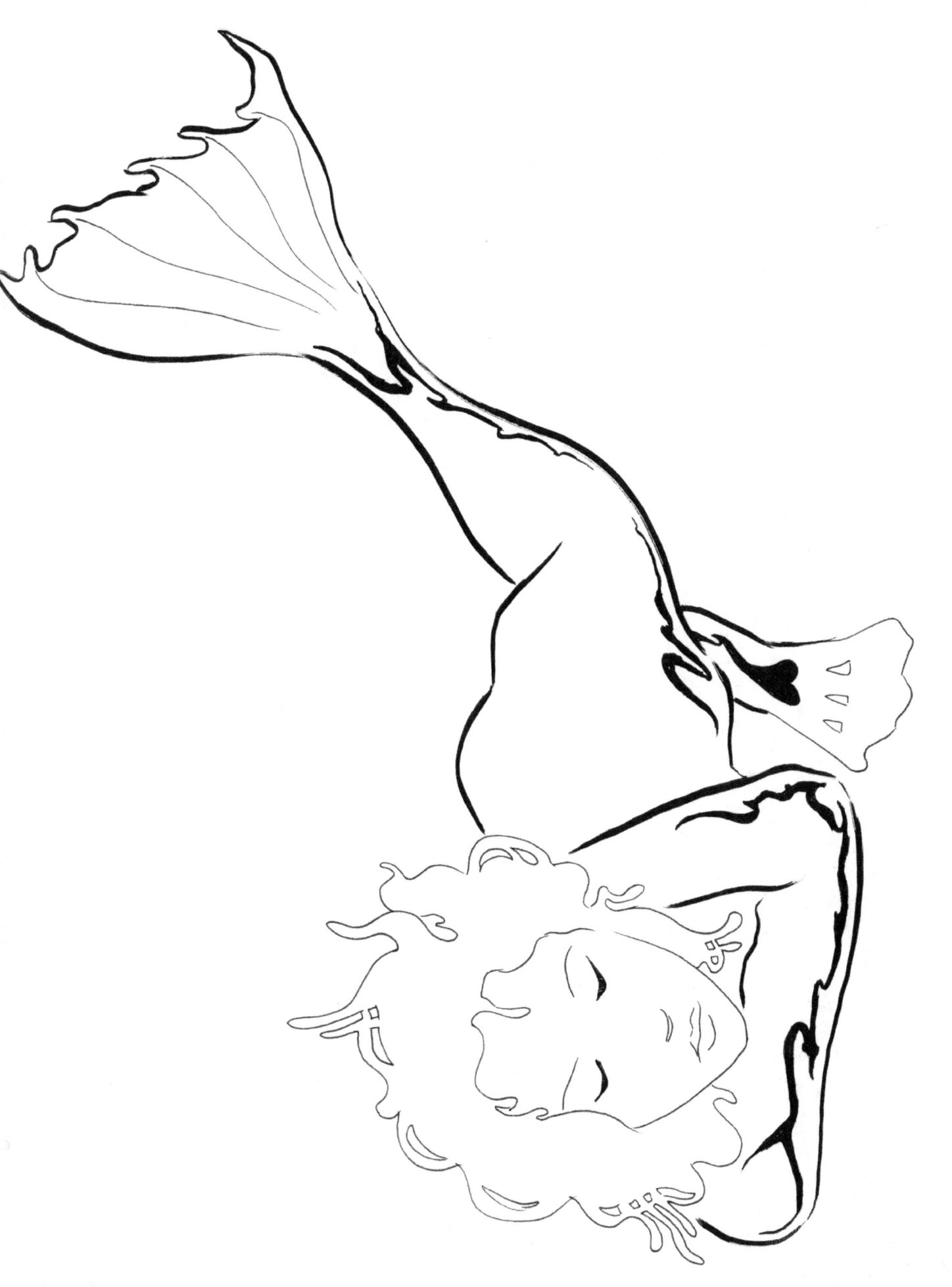

www.ingramcontent.com/pod-product-compliance
Lightning Source LLC
Chambersburg PA
CBHW062235220526
45471CB00009B/3487